CONTINUUM

Black Literature Journal
Volume 1, Number 1

Willow Books
A Division of Aquarius Press

www.WillowLit.net

CONTINUUM: Black Literature Journal

Volume 1, Number 1

Editor: Randall Horton

Cover design: Aquarius Press

ISBN 978-0-9971996-6-6

Willow Books, a Division of Aquarius Press

www.WillowLit.net

Printed in the United States of America

Contents

NIKKI GIOVANNI

Nikki Giovanni was an American poet whose writings range from calls for black power to poems for children. Giovanni wrote more than two dozen books, including volumes of poetry, illustrated children's books and three collections of essays. Books include *Bicycles* (Poems), *Chasing Utopia (Poems)*, *A Good Cry (Poems)* and *Make Me Rain (Poems)*. Giovanni received 30 honorary degrees. She received 21 honorary doctorates and a host of other awards, including Woman of the Year titles from three different magazines and the Governors' Awards in the Arts from both Tennessee and Virginia. *Rosa*, her biography of legendary civil rights activist Rosa Parks, won Caldecott Honors and the Coretta Scott King Medal for best-illustrated book. Other books include the collection of adult poetry *Acolytes* and the novel *On My Journey Now: Looking at African American History Through the Spirituals*. Three of her volumes of poetry—*Love Poems, Blues: For All the Changes,* and Quilting the *Black-Eyed Pea*—were winners of the NAACP Image Award in 1998, 2000, and 2003. Giovanni taught writing and literature at Virginia Tech as a distinguished professor.

No Complaints
(For Gwendolyn Brooks, 1917—2001)

maybe there is something about the seventh of June: Gwen,
Prince and me . . . or maybe people just have to be born at some
time . . . and there are only three hundred sixty-five days or three
sixty-six every four years or so . . . meaning that some things
happen at the same time in the same rising sign . . . and the same
houses in Gemini . . . but some of us might also consider the
possibility of reincarnating revolving restructuring that spirit . . .
reshaping that spirit . . . releasing that spirit . . . tucking the use-
less inside and when the useless pushes out again we restructure
again and poetry and song and praisesong go on . . . because it is
the right thing to do

we always will cry when a great heart . . . a good soul . . . one of
the premier poets of her age restructures . . . reincarnates . . .
revolves into a resolve that we now carry in our hearts . . . as all

great women and men are alive . . . not by biology but remem-
brance . . . and that's all right . . . as the old folk say . . . because as
long as they stay on the lips . . . they nestle in our hearts and those
souls which are planted . . . continue growing . . . until generations
not knowing their touch . . . their voice . . . or even the fact
that some Chicago poets are terrible cooks . . . but always fun
to eat with . . . will tell tales of having met someone who knew
someone who once watched a basketball game . . . in which some
Chicago poet cheered for Seattle at the request of some Virginia
poet who wanted more games . . . while Mr. Blakely was amazed
that a Chicago poet was even watching a game . . . and didn't
we miss him as he slipped away watching baseball . . . and what
a way to go . . . though we then did sort of know . . . that once
gone . . . he would call the woman he loved

and so we come to no more phone calls at six a.m. to chat ...
and no more Benihana when we are all in New York . . . and no
more gossiping and questioning and trying to make sense of a
senseless world . . . no more face-to-face . . . only the poetry which
is a great monument from this Topeka daughter to the world . . .
and yet . . . there can be no complaints in this passing . . . no
sorrow songs . . . no if onlys . . . it is all here: the work the love:
the woman: who gave and gave and gave . . . no complaints of too
long or too hard . . . no injustice of accident or misunderstanding
of disease . . . just one great woman moving to the next phase . . .
and us on the ground . . . giving Alleluias

Rosa Parks

This is for the Pullman Porters who organized when people said
they couldn't. And carried the Pittsburgh Courier and the Chicago
Defender to the Black Americans in the South so they would
know they were not alone. This is for the Pullman Porters who
helped Thurgood Marshall go south and come back north to fight
the fight that resulted in Brown v. Board of Education because
even though Kansas is west and even though Topeka is the birth-
place of Gwendolyn Brooks, who wrote the powerful "The
Chicago Defender Sends a Man to Little Rock," it was the
Pullman Porters who whispered to the traveling men both

the Blues Men and the "Race" Men so that they both would know what was going on. This is for the Pullman Porters who smiled as if they were happy and laughed like they were tickled when some folks were around and who silently rejoiced in 1954 when the Supreme Court announced its 9—0 decision that "separate is inherently unequal." This is for the Pullman Porters who smiled and welcomed a fourteen-year-old boy onto their train in 1955. They noticed his slight limp that he tried to disguise with a doo-wop walk; they noticed his stutter and probably understood why his mother wanted him out of Chicago during the summer when school was out. Fourteen-year-old Black boys with limps and stutters are apt to try to prove themselves in dangerous ways when mothers aren't around to look after them. So this is for the Pullman Porters who looked over that fourteen-year-old while the train rolled the reverse of the Blues Highway from Chicago to St. Louis to Memphis to Mississippi. This is for the men who kept him safe; and if Emmett Till had been able to stay on a train all summer he would have maybe grown a bit of a paunch, certainly lost his hair, probably have worn bifocals and bounced his grandchildren on his knee telling them about his summer riding the rails. But he had to get off the train. And ended up in Money, Mississippi. And was horribly, brutally, inexcusably, and unacceptably murdered. This is for the Pullman Porters who, when the sheriff was trying to get the body secretly buried, got Emmett's body on the northbound train, got his body home to Chicago, where his mother said: I want the world to see what they did to my boy. And this is for all the mothers who cried. And this is for all the people who said Never Again. And this is about Rosa Parks whose feet were not so tired, it had been, after all, an ordinary day, until the bus driver gave her the opportunity to make history. This is about Mrs. Rosa Parks from Tuskegee, Alabama, who was also the field secretary of the NAACP. This is about the moment Rosa Parks shouldered her cross, put her worldly goods aside, was willing to sacrifice her life, so that that young man in Money, Mississippi, who had been so well protected by the Pullman Porters, would not have died in vain. When Mrs. Parks said "NO" a passionate movement was begun. No longer would there be a reliance on the law; there was a higher law. When Mrs. Parks brought that light of hers to expose the evil of the system, the sun came and rested on her shoulders bringing the heat and the light of truth. Others would follow Mrs. Parks. Four young men in Greensboro, North Carolina, would also say No. Great voices would be raised singing the praises of God and exhorting us "to forgive those who trespass against us." But it was the Pullman Porters who safely got Emmett to his granduncle and it was Mrs. Rosa Parks who could not stand that death. And in not being able to stand it. She sat back down.

ISHMAEL REED

Ishmael Reed has written over 30 books of poetry, prose, essays, and plays. He is also an editor of anthologies and magazines, a publisher, television producer, public media commentator, cartoonist, teacher and lecturer. Reed has penned lyrics for musicians ranging from Taj Mahal to Macy Gray. Reed has been the recipient of a MacArthur Grant, has been a Pulitzer finalist, and he has been nominated twice for the National Book Award. Most recently he was named the University of California at Berkeley's Emeritus Professor Awardee of the Year 2020 and honored with the Anisfield-Wolf 2022 Lifetime Achievement Award.

His works include the novel *Mumbo Jumbo*, celebrated in a 50th anniversary edition from Scribner's in 2022, as well as nonfiction, plays and poetry.

Cromwell's Witness

(A friend told Oliver Cromwell, a Black soldier who was honored by George Washington, to come to St. Mary's Episcopal Church, Burlington, New Jersey. One of his children escorted him to the church from his house on Union Street. He was frail and so he has to stop from time to time. His son held him up. He had a painful case of arthritis. Calluses on his feet which make every step hurt. When they entered the church, the gathering of Whites, Blacks, and Oneida shouted, "Surprise." He looked to his son, who smiled. He's was in on the surprise Birthday Party. Cromwell was asked to speak. All of sudden he stood tall. And walked proudly to the front of the room. He was escorted to the pulpit. Some

members of the audience yelled, "Tell us about 1776." "Tell us about Washington." He told them about how hurt he and his fellow comrades-in-arms felt when they found that their enemies, the Hessians, mercenaries from the Netherlands, were receiving better treatment than they, a complaint that Black soldiers have made frequently during American wars.)

After the defeat in New York

September 15, 1776
Those sunshine patriots thought
That we were a goner but the old
Man had other thoughts
        The men were exhausted and
And demoralized after we ran
        With our tails between our legs
        From New York
So I started banging on my drum
        That put a little pep in their
        Step as we marched those
        9 miles to Trenton
        We'd sneaked across the Delaware
        And surprised those Hessians

It was Christmas and the Hessians
        Had been celebrating that's how
        We caught them,
        We got respect when we
        Gave those Hessians a good licking
        Only to find out that
These Hessians would receive
Better treatment than us

> Lived comfortably in private homes
> And when they were marched into
> Philadelphia the citizens fed them
> Even though they brutalized our
> Soldiers and plundered private homes
> And raped little girls
> When sometimes we didn't
> Have enough beans to go
> Around

> The Beloved Commander even
> Offered them land if they'd defect
> While the slaves who fought along
> Side us thought they'd be free
> If they showed their valor on
> The battlefield
> Instead, a lot were sent back
> To their masters even though
> One master refused to accept
> His returning slave because he
> Was too old and so he asked
> A man to sell him
> He sold him for a hundred
> Dollars in Mobile, Alabama

We fought the enemy at Trenton,
Princeton, Brandywine Creek,
Germantown, Monmouth, Short
Hills. Some of us had our legs
Torn off
And they're going to treat us like that?
Maybe some of my Black brothers
Were right
Now some of my brothers scolded
Me for fighting under the flag of
> A man who owned slaves
> He didn't even want us in the

Army until Dunmore promised
Slaves that if they fought with the
British, they'd be free
Well them Hessians liked it
So much that many of them
Settled here
Others went back to Hesse
And brought their families

What kind of nation treats
    The enemy better than it
    Treats its soldiers?

    Washington didn't free his
    Slaves until after his death
    But I didn't fight for Washington
    I fought for the revolution
    But I'll
    Never forget the day when the
    Beloved Commander called me
    Into his camp and gave me the
    Badge of Merit
    He didn't say nothin'. To
    Say he was tightlipped would
    Be an overstatement
    The man didn't have no lips
    (laughter).
    Well, I'm getting tired so
    Maybe I'll end
        (Something gets his attention. A commotion is occurring in
        front of the door leading to the downstairs kitchen. A cake topped
        with 97 candles is rolled into the room. The gathering begins to
        sing "Happy Birthday."Oliver says):

    Well, I'll be damned

The Luckiest People in the World

A hard time for you is not
Having enough kegs for
Your fraternity party, or
Hearing that your luxury cruise
Has been cancelled while
Our ancestors had to go
Without beer and didn't
Come over here on yachts
They weren't part of no regatta
They came in slave ships
And coffin ships

A hard time for you is when
Others are crowding
Out your bandwidth but
Suppose that you were
A Mexican American citizen
Sent across the border because
Herbert Hoover blamed
You for his Depression
Or how about a Guatemalan
Child thrown in a cage
And separated from
Its parents, permanently
If this happened to your Child
You'd be in a rage

If you think things are bad now
Because the price on your
Hi tech stocks dipped
Imagine that you're a Chinese
Girl kidnapped and sold
On the streets of
San Francisco
Its 1860 and the 6 Companies
Let strangers mangle
You for 75 cents

Yet you're upset because
Your spouse's Chanel
Wasn't delivered in
Time for the dog show

What of the other channel
The one taken by
An immigrant in a leaking boat
That was supposed to take him
From Libya to Italy and the
Boat capsizes and all he
Sees are black fins swimming toward
His children
Channel that

Hell, if times get tough
You have Grubhub and
DoorDash or Walmart
Can get you groceries In two hours when you
Reach for Peach Melba
Think of the long
Lines of cars as
People await their food
Allotments and its 95 degrees
and your children didn't
Eat yesterday and you've
Been unemployed for a
Year and the nurses
Working in a the near
By hospital have to
Use trash bags for
Gowns
The government believes
That CoVid is a Chinese
Hoax

If you think you got it bad
Suppose you were an inmate In San Quentin
and CoVid
Is jumping from cell to cell
After having left a nursing Home, the end for those
Who fought two wars and
Survived two depressions
Think of this as you put
Your $100 designer mask over
Your nose and chin

Your daughter has to
Attend a state school because
She was turned down by Princeton?
Girls in other countries
Get acid thrown into their
Faces if found reading books
Or they're too busy
To think about a book
Because they are slaves in India, Africa and cases even
Pop up in the United States
From time to time
Isn't she better off than
Those kidnapped by Boko Haram or
Isis or another group
Of over armed idiots
High on testosterone
Smelling themselves
Roaming the world
Looking for a fight

Americans, even
Though you might
Be led by an over
The hill vaudevillian
Who has a hole in
The sole of his soft
Shoe and streaks of

Makeup on his collar
And lacks grog and Is trailed by a roll
Of toilet paper

As he boards Air Force 1
Even though your
Lead evangelists romp
From motel to motel In their underwear
Even though some
Boy Scout leaders
And some Catholic
Bishops get off on children

Unlike people in the
Rest of the world
Who hold their children
As they starve in their arms
Who drink from water that
Animals and humans defecate
In
Whose lands have become
Deserts and sink under water
Because of your insatiable
Greed for toxic energy
You live a charmed life
You always win the lottery
The daily double
3 bells in a row in Las Vegas
Yet you whine grouse
Bitch and moan when
Your lives are mirrored In the
Streisand song
You are the
The Luckiest People in
The world.

devorah major

devorah major is a California-born "granddaughter of immigrants, documented and undocumented who works as a writer, editor, writing coach, spoken word performer, recording artist, and poetry professor." The Poet-in-Residence of the Fine Arts Museums of San Francisco, major has toured internationally in places such as Northern and Southern Italy, Bosnia, Jamaica, Venezuela, Belgium, England and Wales, and throughout the United States both performing her poetry and serving on panels speaking on African-American poetry, Beat Poetry, and poetry of resistance. In 2015, major premiered her play, *Classic Black: Voices of 19th Century African-Americans* at the S.F. International Arts Festival. Her most recent poetry collection is *califia's daughter* (Willow Books, 2020).

downpressors

Woe to the downpressors:
They'll eat the bread of sorrow! Bob Marley

you walked on our bones for centuries
turned them to sand
poured into sandboxes
for your children to build sandcastles

and when the sand became translucent
filled with the sunlight
burning your eyes
you found more to sacrifice

sent vultures to strip away our skins
and built ladders formed
from our ribs, limbs and skulls
on which you climbed
to get a better view of the lands
you planned to conquer

and now we rise
joined by
some of your children
and grandchildren

who have eaten of shame
and refuse to travel
on the rails you laid
with our bones

and each of you
who blocks our path
tries to press us back
will be blinded by our brilliance
blinded
blinded
blinded by our brilliance

city values

for Kenneth Harding

two dollars
in the city of san francisco
is not quite enough
for a sunday newspaper

but you could get a liter of generic
soda pop and have a bit of change
maybe two large organic apples
or a medium order of fast food fries

one tin of quality black shoe polish
or one condom from a club vending machine
or one thigh with a side at church's chicken

or the life of one cocoa skinned
nineteen year old roughly
trying to become a man-

who for want
of a two dollar bus transfer
was shot in the back of the head

writing love

all i want to write are love poems

in this season of rotting flesh
and hollow bellies
in this year of hidden corpses
and shrapnel graveyards

all i want to write are love poems
to the one whose breath
mixes with mine

for the lips i taste
for the hips i encircle
for the sap i share

all i want to write are love poems

about shining eyes
and sweat's perfume
about promises made and kept
about secrets and fears
shared and revealed

in this year of the buried city
this decade of the hunger crop
this century newly begun yet already
with thousands upon thousands
of limbs torn off
eyes burnt out
hearts eviscerated

all i want to write are love poems

i don't want this job of
recording the children's despair
the mothers' grieving the fathers'

misery the sons' brutalization
the planet's storms and fires

it's all too much for me
my eyes fill with salt and become blurred
and only love poems will make it better
will clear the way

but all around me
these others who i love
in knowing and as strangers
are being murdered or enslaved
starved or tortured
imprisoned or forsaken

and the poems i want to write
evade me until i am left
with nothing but this howl
wedged between my teeth

all i want to write are love poems

about blue kissing my morning
lemons tart and fresh flavoring
my afternoons crescent moons
arching away from venus' sparkle
in a star hungry sky
all i want to write
are love poems

all i want to write
is love

LENARD D. MOORE

Lenard D. Moore is a poet, fiction writer, essayist, book reviewer, public speaker, photographer, and the author and/or editor or co-editor of several books, including *All The Songs We Sing* (Blair, 2020), *The Geography Of Jazz* (Blair, 2020), *One Window's Light* (Unicorn Press, 2017), and *A Temple Looming* (WordTech Editions, 2008). His literary works have appeared in *African American Review, Agni, Callaloo, Colorado Review, North American Review, North Dakota Quarterly, Obsidian, Prairie Schooner* and *Valley Voices*. He is the founder and executive director of the Carolina African American Writers' Collective and co-founder of the Washington Street Writers Group. He is the recipient of several awards, including the North Carolina Award for Literature (2014); Haiku Museum of Tokyo Award (2003, 1994, and 1983); and Margaret Walker Creative Writing Award (1997).

SUMMER BLUES FOR GEORGE FLOYD

I wish you were here for your children
Tall, treelike to guide them
Say I wish you were here for your children
Way up treelike to guide them
You don't know how bad we just hurt
Our nerves sting above the hem

Checked the neighborhood for you
Walked up and down the street
Say I checked the neighborhood for you
Walked up and down the street
But I only found the wind
And summer sun to greet

How must you cope everyday
When your feet are heavy?
Can I still proceed now
Just when your feet are heavy?
You pray for strength and stamp away
Hold the tears like a levee.

Say I wish you were here for your children
Tall, treelike to guide right

Say I wish you were here for your children
Tall, treelike to guide right
You dig how my coping now
Has nerves to sting above all might

Now you dig how my coping
Has nerves to sting above all night

8 HAIKU
for Amiri Baraka

first month of the year—
you transform
into Transbluesency

winter recliner—
you bend language
across borders

snow-glazed night
your words flare
off the page

all the voices
rising from Yugen…
the heater hums

close reading…
I recall your voice
amid the chill

falling temperature…
a student's research paper
on your riffs

frigid shadows—
black pupils stare
from Home

the cold deepens…
the conjuring
of Blues People

HAIKU SEQUENCE
for Sonia Sanchez

your whole notes
wake the dormant trees
the wind's breath

drums thump
pulsing of the heartsong
the opening sky

jazz and haiku
shake loose my skin*
a dusting of pollen

insistent running
of the long river
you're a cappella

my black hands
cupping the sunlight
jacuzzi bubbles
orange lilies bow
your noontime strut
up the sidewalk

rain long gone
I recite the syllables
of your language

evening walk
I catch your riff
in my voice

shake loose my skin is the title of Sonia Sanchez's poetry book.

DENISE NICHOLAS

Denise Nicholas is an actor and writer who has starred in numerous films and TV shows, including *Room 222*, for which she earned three Golden Globe nominations, and *In the Heat of the Night*, for which she also wrote several episodes. She lives in Southern California.

Freshwater Road
(excerpt)

Chapter 3

A hard something landed in Celeste's lap, waking her from a doze. Behind the continuous murmur of voices in the office, typewriter carriages banged, bells sounded, and a radio played. "Sign that. I'll take you to the apartment in a minute. I'm Margo." Celeste grasped the clipboard, frowning up at the short, pretty, blue-eyed white girl with edge-straight blonde hair cut just above her shoulders. By the time she got "hi" to her lips, Margo had pivoted into a small army of coverall-wearing Negro and white young people moving around the airless office/storefront picking up papers, diagramming patterns on a blackboard, sticking pins in a map of Mississippi. Celeste wondered if the pins marked the locations of dead bodies, burned buildings, or some other horrendous occurrence. On the walls, pictures of Martin Luther King, Rosa Parks, Medgar Evers. Through the front windows, she saw that the police cars hadn't moved.

Margo huddled over a mimeograph machine near the back wall with a young dark-skinned guy, she cranking the handle of the old inky cylinder while he caught the copies. Celeste eyed them through slits. The last thing she'd expected in this office was a white girl telling *her* what to do, even fi it was only signing some form. Mississippi *and* the civil rights movement meant pushing two years of Ann Arbor's surrounds of white people to the rear.

Here, both Negro and white student-types were working and talking together in easy familiarity. Hard to tell who was in charge. Serious faces, cigarette smoke spiraling up to the white-tiled ceiling, and music coming from a small radio in the corner, Wolfman Jack's gravel-choked voice punctuating the melodies. It had the feeling of a campus gathering, without the food and alcohol.

Celeste walked to the bulletin board to see the photos of rural-looking Negro people grinning with their arms around overall-wearing student-types. Everyone seemed to be old and young at the same time. And, photo after photo of burned down buildings. She went back to her folding chair.

A ballpoint pen dangled at the end of a thin string attached to the clipboard. A typed page and a carbon under it, the word "release" in caps across the top.

> *In the event of your injury or death, neither you nor your family or heirs to your family have a legal right to sue or to otherwise seek compensation from One Man, One Vote.*

This whole trip was going to break Shuck's heart. Beneath the fine suits, the stingy-brimmed hats, the sleek cars, and the smooth demeanor, Shuck was a race man. But Mississippi was a different story. He'd want to come down here and snatch her back to sanity. She'd better call him soon. He'd need to hear her voice to know that she was OK. Wilamena would more than likely hiss and fume and blame it all on Shuck being a race man, constantly talking about Negro this and Negro that, filling Billy and Celeste's heads with all that Negro-ness. She'd have preferred to have them less anchored in things Negro. More classical music, less jazz, more London and Paris, less Harlem and Chicago. And for sure, less Detroit.

A line of typed dashes stretched across the bottom of the page. Celeste's full name was typed under the line and the dates of her stay in Mississippi. A note at the bottom: *Be sure to send one copy home to a parent or guardian before leaving for your project city.*

Celeste's departure date, the end of Freedom Summer, August 21, was two months away. She might be dead by then—or a hero, a northern agitator hero who'd managed to register an entire town of disenfranchised Negroes. She saw herself as a cross between Joan of Arc and Harriet Tubman, the fires of righteousness flaming in her heart stoked by the news reports that had been coming out of the south for the last three years. Her departure date floated on the paper as if the ink had run out, as if there'd be no leaving Mississippi. She signed on the line and pulled the copy from under the carbon, then slipped it into her book bag. Shuck said your decisions were your own when you crossed from teen to adulthood. Age eighteen marked the beginning of adulthood, but the years between eighteen and twenty-one were a kind of nebulous grace period you were given if you appeared not to have good sense. She'd be twenty in November.

The clatter in the office scaled down as the volunteers filtered out in groups of two and three. When Margo led her out to a 1960 Ford and told her to get into the back seat, the police started their engines, too. Had police cars, lurking around midnight corners, followed the other volunteers when they left? She'd seen enough squad cars on the way from the train station to handle it. Was this the routine or was special attention given to new arrivals? Her suitcase gave her away.

Margo's car stank of decomposing cigarettes and sweaty armpits. Celeste added her own train-funk to the haze of odors. From the dark of the car's backseat she watched the back of Margo's head as they rode through the deserted streets of downtown Jackson. The two police cars followed half a block behind them. More than likely, the police knew when she'd arrived at the train station, knew the volunteers' every move. Already Mississippi felt like a moldy hole, a long dark tunnel without enough fresh air, too much moisture, and no light at the end. This interminable night ranked as one of the longest of Celeste's life. When she checked behind them again, the police cars had disappeared. She wanted to relax, but something told her the effort would be a foolish waste of time.

"If you're with a white person and you get stopped by the police, let the white person do the talking." Margo's pure New York City accent leaned against the slow southern night as she drove well under the speed limit, checking to the right and the left and eyeing the rearview mirror at every intersection. Perspiration slicked her face to a moony shine. A dark bandana covered her blonde hair. "Act like you're the maid getting a ride home from work."

"Are you *serious*?" Celeste rolled her eyes at the back of Margo's head. "Nobody's that dumb, even in the movies." Then, she remembered the porter at the train station. Was he acting servile to survive? To get paid, for sure. Now she wished she hadn't looked at him so harshly. She might find herself bobbing and weaving, shuffling to save her own life before this summer was over. Could she do that? What would it do to her? She tried to follow the thought to its conclusion. And what in God's name would Shuck think about her riding around in the backseat pretending to be somebody's maid? He'd want her to survive, pure and simple. Pride could get her a one-way ticket to a tongue lashing, or a beating—or worse, get her tossed into a fast-moving river.

"You'd be amazed." Margo double-checked her rearview mirror, then accelerated. "Another car fell in behind us when the police cars turned around. He's gone."

Maybe it was still the police but in an unmarked car, Celeste thought.

At the next intersection, Margo slowed. "When it comes to the movement, every white person in the south is the police. They all follow us. There's no real distinction between regular white people and the police down here."

Celeste sank deeper into the backseat, her heart skipping through its beats like a drummer on smack. Margo knew what she was thinking before she'd opened her mouth. She dug her fingers into the crack where the seat meets the seat back and brought her hands out with dirt and lint pieces sticking to her fingers. "So what do I do if I get stopped with all Negro people in the car? Jump out and start tap dancing?"

"You might have to." Margo turned into a residential section of wood-framed houses set back beyond night-black lawns. "It's already happened. Some volunteers were stopped and the cops made them dance in the middle of the highway. Guns drawn."

Celeste's neck tensed as though her vertebrae were fusing. What to say now? Nothing. Just listen. Pay attention. She caught Margo's eyes in the rearview mirror.

"Be respectful and pray. Sing freedom songs in your head. By the end of orientation, you'll know the words to a lot of 'em." Margo let her eyes go back to scanning as they moved quietly through the streets.

No lamps lit the windows, no porch lights were on, and the shrubs and hedges were just dark shapes in the night. Not even the trees moved, just the car gliding in slow motion over the black tar. Celeste ducked her head well below the back window, gasping for air, legs sprawled across the bump, peering out like a child. She tasted again the train coffee and that mayonnaisy ham sandwich from the shop in Memphis.

Margo turned into what looked like a housing project of low, dark-brick buildings. "Try to get the name of the officer stopping you. The patrol car number, details that can be reported to the FBI. Try to stay calm. Try to stay alive."

Celeste bucked herself up a bit, and pushed aside her bristling self-consciousness at being a trainee with a white-girl boss who obviously knew more about staying alive in Mississippi than she did.

"Remember names and squad car numbers. Sing the words to freedom songs," Margo repeated. "As soon as I get you ready for Pineyville and the other straggler ready for the Delta, I'm going to Aberdeen." Margo put her arm on the car window ledge, the warm air fluttering her bandana. She looked so in control, she made it sound like they were off to be camp counselors.

Celeste strained to sense Margo's fear. maybe she was so afraid herself, no one else's fear had a chance. She glared beyond the car's front lights. "Pineyville? Where's that?" She checked the map of Mississippi in her mind. Greenwood, Vicksburg, Natchez, Yazoo City. Names like dreams that pillowed nightmares.

"Down below Hattiesburg, a few miles from the Louisiana border." Margo stopped the car in front of an apartment building with windows across the front, then turned off the engine and the lights. The engine ticked down to nothing. "Used to be the Piney Woods before the loggers cut down all the trees." She sat low in her seat but alert, head turning like a radar scanner. "The Gulf coast is nice, but it's still Mississippi, and when it's not, it's Louisiana or Alabama or Florida. Same goddamned thing."

How much farther *down below* could they go? Where did Mississippi end? Celeste stopped a moan that formed in her throat, and said, "Aren't you afraid?" She didn't want to be the only one afraid.

"Yeah." Margo turned a little in the car seat and looked directly at her, and Celeste saw a wide-eyed girl very much like herself. They were about the same age. They had come to Mississippi for the same reason. "Only a nut wouldn't be afraid in this place."

Celeste sighed, thanked God she wasn't alone. "That helps."

The shrieking of cicadas and mole crickets swelled, aroused by the sound of the car, the low-talking voices. Nothing romantic about it. No harking back to benign nighttime stories of the sounds of the south, no animated crickets and puffy-haired Negroes with smiles and songs on their lips. This was a tunnel of death. Her mouth tasted like sandpaper. Then, suddenly, the quiet mushroomed around them. Celeste heard her own heart beating. All she could see were dark trees, hedges near windowpanes lit only by the reflected moon. She sat up a bit to see the surrounding area.

"Stay low." Margo's voice was sharp. "There's a car under the trees across the street. It's always there." Margo turned to Celeste and smiled a creepy smile in the soupy darkness. "The Klan shot out the street lights when they found out we were housing volunteers here. We think that's one of their cars."

Celeste glared at the car, caught between wanting to thump Margo on the back of the head for scolding her like she was a child and being thankful that Margo had warned her about the lurking danger. Nothing moved inside the dark car. Just black windows and no heads.

"How long've you been here?" Celeste's voice crackled between her true voice and the hoarse whisper of fear.

Margo pulled a single key out of her bag and held it up in the streak of moonlight coming through the front windshield. "Six months." She sounded proud. Celeste didn't want to look up to a white girl, but she had sense enough to know that Margo had already passed tests that she hadn't even studied for. She had to give Margo her due, relax inside for a moment, and listen to her as she would her teacher.

"For the next few days, you go through nonviolence training with the stragglers. Y'all are the last group. We need to get you going to your projects so you'll have time to do what we're here to do." Firm-voiced, Margo laid it out, though the "ya'll" was a tight fit with her New York accent. "You'll be running your freedom school and your voting project at the same time. The voter education classes take priority. That's pretty much it. Oh, and try not to get killed." Straight faced and no nonsense. She handed the single key to Celeste and indicated with a nod that it was time for Celeste to get out of the car.

Fear approaching terror hurtled through Celeste. She opened the door and hunched over to climb out of the backseat. The civil rights demonstrations on campus seemed so harmless. That was another world. This was the real deal. Run a freedom school and try not to get killed.

She'd read it in her packet of materials, knew the school was a part of the summer project, couldn't remember precisely what she was supposed to do. She needed to sleep, to bathe, to eat a meal that had a green vegetable on the plate. Negro people were *her* people. She didn't want a white girl from New York to be more courageous on their behalf than she was. She had to submit, though, because it might be the difference between life and death. Mississippi wasn't Ann Arbor or Detroit, and she needed to keep that foremost in her mind.

"Your contact's Reverend Singleton." Margo never stopped scoping the darkness, even as she leaned across the front seat and talked to Celeste out of the car window. A real soldier. "He's the point man in Pineyville. I'll fill you in over the next few days."

Celeste tried to gather up some mettle for her cracking, slipping voice. She leaned down, head in the window, wanting to crawl through the window back into the car. "When do I go?"

"As soon as I see you're ready. Stay low to the floor at night. That apartment's been shot into. Grab the empty mattress. There's another volunteer in there."

Celeste hefted her suitcase and book bag out of the back seat, wondering how long it would take her to get ready. Ready for what? Nonviolence training, of course. Practice being oppressed, practice not getting killed. Taking low to keep the peace, removing chips from shoulders, anger from lips, history from heart. She lingered by the side of the car, afraid to walk through open space. Afraid she'd end up like Medgar Evers, shot dead a few feet from his front door. Across the street, the dark car waited. "What about the police?" Celeste heard her own dumb question too late to pull it back. They'd just been followed by the police. The police were all over Jackson waiting.

"Forget the police." Margo sighed on the verge of impatience. "I'll pick y'all up in the morning. White volunteers have to sleep in another unit. No integrating. Not yet anyway." She started the car, staying low, her parchment-white face surrounded by her dark bandana and the night. "I'll wait 'til you're in the door. Go on."

Celeste hunched over and scurried for the door as Margo started the engine. her suitcase and book bag scraped along the walkway. She might've crawled on her hands and knees, anything to not be a walking target. She found the door knob and felt around for the keyhole, then finally got the door open. When she turned around, Margo gave her a quick wave and headed, it seemed, almost directly for the dark car across the street, going so slowly it seemed to be a taunt.

A miniature lamp sat on the floor next to the mattress but barely lit the dark corner of the living room. Two folded sheets and a flat pillow with no case lay on top. In Ann Arbor, Celeste's mattress was on the floor, too, but not because it had to be, not because someone might shoot at her through the windows. She positioned her suitcase and book bag at the end of the mattress to form a footboard, or at least a blockade, then undressed down to her underwear before pulling a light cotton nightgown over her dirty body, keeping low the whole time. The jumper and the blouse were going in the bottom of her suitcase, never to be seen again until she got home. No, better to air out the sweaty clothes before putting them into her suitcase. She laid them on the wood floor. To take a bath or even to just wash up in the face bowl meant turning on lights, which would locate her for the mystery men across the street in the dark car.

She sat on the mattress and leaned against the wall staring at the small, bare living room. Always she had a sense of waiting. It went way back. Waiting for Wilamena to shower her with the hugs and kisses she saw other children receive from their mothers, waiting for Shuck to pick her and her brother up from some relative's house, waiting for Shuck's numbers to fall. Waiting for her life to begin. Now she'd begin her own journey with no clue as to how it would end.

"Your name better be Celeste." The voice wavered, followed by the padding of bare feet on wood. "Otherwise, I'm going out the bedroom window."

"It is," Celeste called in a whisper. She had hoped the other volunteer would be sleeping, giving her time to just sit there and mull over the possibilities of what lay ahead.

"Good." A door closed and in seconds there was the sound of a flushing toilet. A young woman crept into the living room, walking squatted down. "Ramona Clark."

Ramona sat down on the floor and leaned back against the door frame. Her hair was a mass of wooly kinks, round like an upside down bowl. Celeste could make out a small brown face, big oval eyes. "Haven't slept since I got here."

"Celeste Tyree." She felt her dirty, frizzled, humidity-inflated curls and waves, every strand symbolic of a contorted family tree. "That car across the street might keep anybody from sleeping."

"Amen to that." Ramona said. "Where're you from?"

"Michigan. Detroit. Actually, I'm in school in Ann Arbor." She tried to see more of Ramona's face in the dim light.

Ramona's head moved back and forth, her big bowl of kinky hair swaying. "Ooo wee. Not many black folks up there."

"Not many." Celeste heard the "black." Speakers from the movement who came to campus said it too. She hoped Ramona wasn't excluding her, tossing her in the "other" pile—the "good hair" pile, the light-eyed Negro pile. Negroes used to be "colored." Kids used to fight over being called black. It was the new title, the new calling. Black folks. She wanted to be in it. Shuck would be. Wilamena wouldn't. Celeste herself hadn't gotten comfortable saying "black."

"I'm at Howard with the black intelligentsia, the so called 'high-yellow first line of defense,' no offense intended." Ramona's voice eased out, consonants hit then released very quickly, sliding softly off the edges of the words.

Celeste bristled and lied. "None taken." Shuck was in her head telling her there was no high yellow, no low yellow, or anything else. There was just Negroes. Now, just black folks. Period. Celeste gave herself a point. Shuck was always ahead of the pack, in the vanguard. And she always trying to catch up.

"Where're they sending you?" Ramona stretched her legs out on the wood floor.

"Someplace called Pineyville." All she could see was the bowl of hair and flashes of the whites of Ramona's eyes. "I never even *heard* of it."

"Boy, you hit the jackpot." Ramona's eyes flared wide. "That's where they lynched Leroy Boyd James."

"Jesus." Celeste's train-weary mouth dried like dusty bones. She'd never heard of Leroy Boyd James, either.

"It was in the fifties. I did a paper on lynching in three deep-south states since World War II. I'm a sociology major." Ramona leaned her head back against the door jamb.

Every Negro in America was a sociology major, like it or not, college or not. You had to be. "What happened to him?" Celeste knew before Ramona said a word.

"They say he raped a white woman. Never got to court. Got kidnapped from the jail down there, beaten, shot, and dumped into the Pearl River. The sheriff said it never happened. A fisherman pulled him out. Body got caught on some tree roots or something. Otherwise, he'd have been swept down to the Gulf by the currents. Disappeared. A prisoner told the FBI that the sheriff there opened the door to some men. Nobody was charged with his murder."

All the air sighed out of Celeste's body. This wanting to know could definitely give you nightmares. Maybe Ramona exaggerated. Maybe there was more to the story, but she couldn't fathom what that might be. She'd seen the photos of Emmett Till. She'd seen the range of horror when it came to white women and Negro men. She'd tried to stir up enough saliva in her mouth to swallow. Where're they sending you?"

"Indianola. In the Delta." Ramona sighed. "Plantation country."

Wasn't Mississippi *all* plantation country? And what was Pineyville? A lot more than the Piney Woods, evidently. Leroy Boyd James. A new wrench of fear cranked her stomach, sent the acids churning and the ghost of that ham sandwich flying.

"You running your project by yourself?"

"Unless some more volunteers show up. They've got a pretty active bunch of black folks int eh town." Ramona got into her squat-walk position. "Oh, the lady across the way brings biscuits and jelly in the morning. We've got coffee. The phone in the hall is for emergencies. They said we can call collect anywhere. The FBI numbers are right next to the phone there." Ramona disappeared around the corner. "I hope *you* can sleep. I sure can't. Don't forget to stay low."

"Goodnight." Celeste shriveled down the wall, legs spread out on the mattress. She felt like she'd been awake for days. Too many thoughts swirled in her head.

Sporadic dog barks, crickets, the creaking of tress..No low music in the background. No laughing voices with conversation riffs in between. It had to be three in the morning by now. A thickness in the air that made you think you were hearing things, but when you really pressed your ears to it, there was nothing there.

Celeste squat-walked to the open front windows, sat down on the hard-wood floor, and pushed on the screens. They were locked in place. Light-colored curtains waited for a breeze, any slight shuffle of air. The car across the street glimmered in a sliver of moonlight. Ghosts with guns. Sweat bubbled out on her forehead, under her arms, between her legs. She smelled her own body, the dampness curdling into a pungent aroma.

She crawled back to the mattress. The heavy air weighted her down on the thin bed, the hardness of the floor rising into her spine. What had Leroy Boyd James really done? Was it like Emmett Till? A whistle, a nothing whistle? She knew there were white girls in Ann Arbor who loved the easy grace of long dark arms and lips that felt like pillows in heaven. But this wasn't Ann Arbor. Margo standing at the mimeo machine with that guy? What was that about? Maybe nothing. Margo was from New York. No big deal. But where was he from? He's the one who'd pay the price. Down here, death came hunting when you reached across the lines of demarcation. In Ann Arbor, maybe just a hateful look, a bad name slung across some busy street. She and J.D. turned heads. Here, crossed love got dropped in the cracks of old storm shelters, locked away with warning signs marked Danger. People died for flirting. She'd read enough to know this was the real deal. Mary Evans's voice in her head, *You be careful, girl, you hear? Miss'sippi ain't nothing to play with.*

James Baldwin

James Baldwin was an essayist, playwright, novelist and voice of the American civil rights movement known for works including *Notes of a Native Son*, *The Fire Next Time* and *Go Tell It on the Mountain*. Writer and playwright James Baldwin published the 1953 novel *Go Tell It on the Mountain*, receiving acclaim for his insights on race, spirituality and humanity. Other novels included *Giovanni's Room*, *Another Country* and *Just Above My Head*.

Amen

No, I don't feel death coming.
I feel death going:
having thrown up his hands,
for the moment.
I feel like I know him
better than I did.
Those arms held me,
for a while,
and, when we meet again,
there will be that secret knowledge
between us.

Blues for Mister Charlie (Excerpt)

NOTES FOR BLUES

THIS PLAY HAS BEEN on my mind—has been bugging me—for several years.

It is unlike anything else I've ever attempted in that I remember vividly the first time it occurred to me; for in fact, it did not occur to me, but to Elia Kazan. Kazan asked me at the end of 1958 if I would be interested in working in the Theatre. It was a generous offer, but I did not react with great enthusiasm because I did not then, and don't now, have much respect for what goes on in the American Theatre. I am not convinced that it is a Theatre; it seems to me a series, merely, of commercial speculations, stale, repetitious, and timid. I certainly didn't see much future for me in that frame-work, and I was profoundly unwilling to risk my morale and my talent—my life—in endeavors which could only increase a level of frustration already dangerously high.

Nevertheless, the germ of the play persisted. It is based, very distantly indeed, on the case of Emmett Till—the Negro youth who was murdered in Mississippi in 1955. The murderer in this case was acquitted. (His brother, who helped him do the deed, is now a deputy sheriff in Rulesville, Mississippi.) After his acquittal, he recounted the facts of the murder—for one cannot refer to his performance as a confession—to William Bradford Huie, who wrote it all down in an article called "Wolf Whistle." I do not know why the case pressed on my mind so hard— but it would not let me go. I absolutely dreaded committing myself to writing a play—there were enough people around already telling me that I couldn't write novels—but I began to see that my fear of the form masked a much deeper fear. That fear was that I would never be able to draw a valid portrait of the murderer. In life, obviously, such people baffle and terrify me and, with one part of my mind at least, I hate them and would be willing to kill them. Yet, with another part of my mind, I am aware that no man is a villain in his own eyes. Something in the man knows—must know—that what he is doing is evil; but in order to accept the knowledge the man would have to change. What is ghastly and really almost hopeless in our racial situation now is that the crimes we have committed are so great and so unspeakable that the acceptance of this knowledge would lead, literally, to madness. The human being, then, in order to protect himself, closes his eyes, compulsively repeats his crimes, and enters a spiritual darkness which no one can describe.

But if it is true, and I believe it is, that all men are brothers, then we have the duty to try to understand this wretched man; and while we probably cannot hope to liberate him, begin working toward the liberation of his children. For we, the American people, have created him, he is our servant; it is we who put the cattle-prodder in his hands, and we are responsible for the crimes that he commits. It is we who have locked him in the prison of his color. It is we who have persuaded him that Negroes are worthless human beings, and that it is his sacred duty, as a white man, to protect the honor and purity of his tribe. It is we who have forbidden him, on pain of exclusion from the tribe, to accept his beginnings, when he and black people loved each other, and rejoice in them, and use them; it is we who have made it mandatory—honorable—that white father should deny black son.

These are grave crimes indeed, and we have committed them and continue to commit them in order to make money.

The play then, for me, takes place in Plaguetown, U.S.A., now. The plague is race, the plague is our concept of Christianity: and this raging plague has the power to destroy every human relationship. I once took a short trip with Medgar Evers to the back-woods of Mississippi. He was investigating the murder of a Negro man by a white storekeeper which had taken place months before. Many people talked to Medgar that night, in dark cabins, with their lights out, in whispers; and we had been followed for many miles out of Jackson, Mississippi, not by a lunatic with a gun, but by state troopers. I will never forget that night, as I will never forget Medgar—who took me to the plane the next day. We promised to see each other soon. When he died, something entered into me which I cannot describe, but it was then that I resolved that nothing under heaven would prevent me from getting this play done. We are walking in terrible darkness here, and this is one man's attempt to bear witness to the reality and the power of light.

James Baldwin
New York, April, 1964

Cast of Characters

Meridian Henry, a black man and minister in a small town in the American South
Richard Henry, Meridian's son
Lyle Britten, store owner who is suspected of killing Richard
Josephine Britten, Lyle's wife
Parnell James, editor of the town's newspaper
Juanita, a student
Joel Davis, "Papa D," a bar owner

ACT I

MULTIPLE SET, the skeleton of which, in the first two acts, is the Negro church, and, in the third act, the courthouse. The church and the courthouse are on opposite sides of a southern street; the audience should always be aware, during the first two acts, of the dome of the courthouse and the American flag. During the final act, the audience should always be aware of the steeple of the church, and the cross.

The church is divided by an aisle. The street door upstage faces the audience. The pulpit is downstage, at an angle, so that the minister is simultaneously addressing the congregation and the audience. In the third act, the pulpit is replaced by the witness stand.

This aisle also functions as the division between WHITETOWN and BLACKTOWN. The action among the blacks takes place on one side of the stage, the action among the whites on the opposite side of the stage—

which is to be remembered during the third act, which takes place, of course, in a segregated courtroom.

This means that RICHARD's room, LYLE's store, PAPA D.'s joint, JO's kitchen, etc., are to exist principally by suggestion, for these shouldn't be allowed to obliterate the skeleton, or, more accurately, perhaps, the framework, suggested above.

For the murder scene, the aisle functions as a gulf. The stage should be built out, so that the audience reacts to the enormity of this gulf, and so that RICHARD, when he falls, falls out of sight of the audience, like a stone, into the pit.

In the darkness we hear a shot.

Lights up slowly on LYLE, staring down at the ground. He looks around him, bends slowly and picks up RICHARD's body as though it were a sack. He carries him upstage drops him.

LYLE: And may every nigger like this nigger end like this nigger—face down in the weeds!

(Exits. BLACKTOWN: The church. A sound of mourning begins. Meridian, Tom, Ken and Arthur.)

MERIDIAN: No, no, no! You have to say it like you mean it—the way they really say it: nigger, nigger, nigger! Nigger! Tom, the way you saying it, it sounds like you just might want to make friends. And that's not the way they sound out there. Remember all that's happened.

Remember we having a funeral here—tomorrow night. Remember why. Go on, hit it again.

TOM: You dirty nigger, you no-good black bastard, what you doing down here, anyway?

MERIDIAN: That's much better. Much, much better. Go on.

TOM: Hey, boy, where's your mother? I bet she's lying up in bed, just a-pumping away, ain't she, boy?

MERIDIAN: That's the way they sound!

TOM: Hey, boy, how much does your mother charge? How much does your sister charge?

KEN: How much does your wife charge?

MERIDIAN: Now you got it. You really got it now. That's them. Keep walking, Arthur. Keep walking!

TOM: You get your ass off these streets from around here, boy, or we going to do us some cutting—we're going to cut that big, black thing off of you, you hear?

MERIDIAN: Why you all standing around there like that? Go on and get you a nigger. Go on!

(A scuffle.)

MERIDIAN: All right. All right! Come on, now. Come on.

(Ken steps forward and spits in Arthurs face.) ARTHUR: You black s.o.b., what the hell do you think you're doing? You mother—!

MERIDIAN: Hey, hold it! Hold it! Hold it!

(Meridian wipes the boy's face. They are all trembling.) (Mother Henry enters.)

MOTHER HENRY: Here they come. And it looks like they had a time.

(Juanita, Lorenzo, Pete, Jimmy, al Negro, carry placards, enter, exhausted and disheveled, wounded; Pete is weeping. The placards bear such legends as Freedom Now, We Want The Murderer, One Man, One Vote, etc.)

JUANITA: We shall overcome!

LORENZO: We shall not be moved! (Laughs) We were moved tonight, though. Some of us has been moved to tears.

MERIDIAN: Juanita, what happened?

JUANITA: Oh, just another hometown Saturday night.

MERIDIAN: Come on, Pete, come on, old buddy. Stop it. Stop it.

LORENZO: I don't blame him. I do not blame the cat. You feel like a damn fool standing up there, letting them white mothers beat on your ass

—shoot, if I had my way, just once—stop crying, Pete, goddammit!

JUANITA: Lorenzo, you're in church.

LORENZO: Yeah. Well, I wish to God I was in an arsenal. I'm sorry, Meridian, Mother Henry—I don't mean that for you. I don't understand you. I don't understand Meridian here. It was his son, it was your grandson, Mother Henry, that got killed, butchered! Just last week, and yet, here you sit—in this—this—the house of this damn almighty God who don't care what happens to nobody, unless, of course, they're white. Mother Henry, I got a lot of respect for you and all that, and for Meridian, too, but that white man's God is white. It's that damn white God that's been lynching us and burning us and castrating us and raping our women and robbing us of everything that makes a man a man for all these hundreds of years. Now, why we sitting around here, in His house? If I could get my hands on Him, I'd pull Him out of heaven and drag Him through this town at the end of a rope.

MERIDIAN: No, you wouldn't.

LORENZO: I wouldn't? Yes, I would. Oh, yes, I would.

JUANITA: And then you wouldn't be any better than they are.

LORENZO: I don't want to be better than they are, why should I be better than they are? And better at what? Better at being a doormat, better at being a corpse? Sometimes I just don't know. We've been demonstrating— non-violently—for more than a year now and all that's happened is that now they'll let us into that crummy library downtown which was obsolete in 1897 and where nobody goes anyway; who in this town reads books? For that we paid I don't know how many thousands of dollars in fines, Jerome is still in the hospital, and we all know that Ruthie is never again going to be the swinging little chick she used to be. Big deal. Now we're picketing that great movie palace downtown where I wouldn't go on a bet; I can live without Yul Brynner and Doris Day, thank you very much.

And we still can't get licensed to be electricians or plumbers, we still can't walk through the park, our kids still can't use the swimming pool in town. We still can't vote, we can't even get registered. Is it worth it? And these people trying to kill us, too? And we ain't even got no guns. The cops ain't going to protect us. They call up the people and tell them where we are and say, "Go get them! They ain't going to do nothing to you—they just dumb niggers!"

MERIDIAN: Did they arrest anybody tonight?

PETE: No, they got their hands full now, trying to explain what Richard's body was doing in them weeds.

LORENZO: It was wild. You know, all the time we was ducking them bricks and praying to God we'd get home before somebody got killed— (Laughs) I had a jingle going through my mind, like if I was a white man, dig? and I had to wake up every morning singing to myself, "Look at the happy nigger, he doesn't give a damn, thank God I'm not a nigger—"

TOGETHER: "—Good Lord, perhaps I am!"

JUANITA: You've gone crazy, Lorenzo. They've done it. You have been unfitted for the struggle.

MERIDIAN: I cannot rest until they bring my son's murderer to trial. That man who killed my son.

LORENZO: But he killed a nigger before, as I know all of you know.

Nothing never happened. Sheriff just shovelled the body into the ground and forgot about it.

MERIDIAN: Parnell will help me.

PETE: Meridian, you know that Mister Parnell ain't going to let them arrest his ass-hole buddy. I'm sorry, Mother Henry!

MOTHER HENRY: That's all right, son.

MERIDIAN: But I think that Parnell has proven to be a pretty good friend to all of us. He's the only white man in this town who's ever really stuck his neck out in order to do—to do right. He's fought to bring about this trial—I can't tell you how hard he's fought. If it weren't for him, there'd be much less hope.

LORENZO: I guess I'm just not as nice as you are. I don't trust as many people as you trust.

MERIDIAN: We can't afford to become too distrustful, Lorenzo.

LORENZO: We can't afford to be too trusting, either. See, when a white man's a good white man, he's good because he wants you to be good. Well, sometimes I just might want to be bad. I got as much right to be bad as anybody else.

MERIDIAN: No, you don't.

LORENZO: Why not?

MERIDIAN: Because you know better.

(Parnell enters.)

PARNELL: Hello, my friends. I bring glad tidings of great joy. Is that the way the phrase goes, Meridian?

JUANITA: Parnell!

PARNELL: I can't stay. I just came to tell you that a warrant's being issued for Lyle's arrest.

JUANITA: They're going to arrest him? Big Lyle Britten? I'd love to know how you managed that.

PARNELL: Well, Juanita, I am not a good man, but I have my little ways.

JUANITA: And a whole lot of folks in this town, baby, are not going to be talking to you no more, for days and days and days.

PARNELL: I hope that you all will. I may have no other company. I think I should go to Lyle's house to warn him. After all, I brought it about and he is a friend of mine—and then I have to get the announcement into my paper.

JUANITA: So it is true.

PARNELL: Oh, yes. It's true.

MERIDIAN: When is he being arrested?

PARNELL: Monday morning. Will you be up later, Meridian? I'll drop by if you are—if I may.

MERIDIAN: Yes. I'll be up.

PARNELL: All right, then. I'll trundle by. Good night all. I'm sorry I've got to run.

MERIDIAN: Good night.

JUANITA: Thank you, Parnell.

PARNELL: Don't thank me, dear Juanita. I only acted—as I believed I had to act. See you later, Meridian.

(Parnel exits.)

MERIDIAN: I wonder if they'll convict him.

JUANITA: Convict him. Convict him. You're asking for heaven on earth.

After all, they haven't even arrested him yet. And, anyway—why should they convict him? Why him? He's no worse than all the others. He's an honorable tribesman and he's defended, with blood, the honor and purity of his tribe!

(WHITETOWN: Lyle holds his infant son up above his head.) LYLE: Hey old pisser. You hear me, sir? I expect you to control your bladder like a gentleman whenever your Papa's got you on his knee.

(Jo enters.)

He got a mighty big bladder, too, for such a little fellow.

JO: I'll tell the world he didn't steal it.

LYLE: You mighty sassy tonight.

(Hands her the child.)

Ain't that right, old pisser? Don't you reckon your Mama's getting kind of sassy? And what do you reckon I should do about it?

(Jo is changing the child's diapers.)

JO: You tell your Daddy he can start sleeping in his own bed nights instead of coming grunting in here in the wee small hours of the morning.

LYLE: And you tell your Mama if she was getting her sleep like she should be, so she can be alert every instant to your needs, little fellow, she wouldn't know what time I come—grunting in.

JO: I got to be alert to your needs, too. I think.

LYLE: Don't you go starting to imagine things. I just been over to the store. That's all.

JO: Till three and four o'clock in the morning?

LYLE: Well, I got plans for the store, I think I'm going to try to start branching out, you know, and I been—making plans.

JO: You thinking of branching out now? Why, Lyle, you know we ain't hardly doing no business now. Weren't for the country folks come to town every Saturday, I don't know where we'd be. This ain't no time to be branching out. We barely holding on.

LYLE: Shoot, the niggers'll be coming back, don't you worry. They'll get over this foolishness presently. They already weary of having to drive forty-fifty miles across the state line to get their groceries—a lot of them ain't even got cars.

JO: Those that don't have cars have friends with cars.

LYLE: Well, friends get weary, too. Joel come in the store a couple of days ago—

JO: Papa D.? He don't count. You can always wrap him around your little finger.

LYLE: Listen, will you? He come in the store a couple of days ago to buy a sack of flour and he told me, he say, The niggers is tired running all over creation to put some food on the table. Ain't nobody going to keep on driving no forty-fifty miles to buy no sack of flour—what you mean when you say Joel don't count?

JO: I don't mean nothing. But there's something wrong with anybody when his own people don't think much of him.

LYLE: Joel's got good sense, is all. I think more of him than I think of a lot of white men, that's a fact. And he knows what's right for his people, too.

JO (Puts son in crib): Well. Selling a sack of flour once a week ain't going to send this little one through college, neither. (A pause) In what direction were you planning to branch out?

LYLE: I was thinking of trying to make the store more—well, more colorful. Folks like color—

JO: You mean, niggers like color.

LYLE: Dammit, Jo, I ain't in business just to sell to niggers! Listen to me, can't you? I thought I'd dress it up, get a new front, put some neon signs in—and, you know, we got more space in there than we use.

Well, why don't we open up a line of ladies' clothes? Nothing too fancy, but I bet you it would bring in a lot more business.

JO: I don't know. Most of the ladies I know buy their clothes at Benton's, on Decatur Street.

LYLE: The niggers don't—anyway, we could sell them the same thing.

The white ladies, I mean—

JO: No. It wouldn't be the same.

LYLE: Why not? A dress is a dress.

JO: But it sounds better if you say you got it on Decatur Street! At Benton's. Anyway—where would you get the money for this branching out?

LYLE: I can get a loan from the bank. I'll get old Parnell to co-sign with me, or have him get one of his rich friends to co-sign with me.

JO: Parnell called earlier—you weren't at the store today.

LYLE: What do you mean, I wasn't at the store?

JO: Because Parnell called earlier and said he tried to get you at the store and that there wasn't any answer.

LYLE: There wasn't any business. I took a walk.

JO: He said he's got bad news for you.

LYLE: What kind of bad news?

JO: He didn't say. He's coming by here this evening to give it to you himself.

LYLE: What do you think it is?

JO: I guess they're going to arrest you?

LYLE: No, they ain't. They ain't gone crazy.

JO: I think they might. We had so much trouble in this town lately and it's been in all the northern newspapers—and now, this—this dead boy—

LYLE: They ain't got no case.

JO: No. But you was the last person to see that crazy boy—alive. And now everybody's got to thinking again—about that other time.

LYLE: That was self defense. The Sheriff said so himself. Hell, I ain't no murderer. They're just some things I don't believe is right.

JO: Nobody never heard no more about the poor little girl—his wife.

LYLE: No. She just disappeared.

JO: You never heard no more about her at all?

LYLE: How would I hear about her more than anybody else? No, she just took off—I believe she had people in Detroit somewhere. I reckon that's where she went.

JO: I felt sorry for her. She looked so lost those last few times I saw her, wandering around town—and she was so young. She was a pretty little thing.

LYLE: She looked like a pickaninny to me. Like she was too young to be married. I reckon she was too young for him.

JO: It happened in the store.

LYLE: Yes.

JO: How people talked! That's what scares me now.

LYLE: Talk don't matter. I hope you didn't believe what you heard.

JO: A lot of people did. I reckon a lot of people still do.

LYLE: You don't believe it?

JO: No. (A pause) You know—Monday morning—we'll be married one whole year!

LYLE: Well, can't nobody talk about us. That little one there ain't but two months old.

(The door bell rings.)

JO: That's Parnell.

(Exits.)

Mark Allan Davis

Mark Allan Davis is a native New Yorker ARTivist for the liberation of all oppressed people, and is an accomplished director, producer, choreographer, actor, playwright, and a fist-pumping troubadour for the labor movement. He is a member of the original Broadway production of the hit musical *The Lion King* and can be heard on its Grammy® Award-winning cast recording. While living abroad in Europe, he traveled, taught, and created many works with his dance theatre company Les Danses Dønsk, and choreographed three feature films. He has written several plays including *The Last Blues of the Empress,* a ghost story about the mysterious disappearance of songs Bessie Smith penned before her tragic death in 1937 and includes seven original songs, and *Pantheon's Edge,* a historical drama examining the relationship between James Baldwin and Lorraine Hansberry, and their fateful meeting with Bobby Kennedy during the last 18 months of her abbreviated life. He recently produced and is the subject of the award-winning film *Before the After,* becoming the 2024 Best U.S. Documentary Short at the Austin International Arts Festival, as well as producing *Monumental Reckoning: Juneteenth 2024 LIVE in Golden Gate Park* with friend and sculptor Dana King and San Francisco's Recreation & Parks Department. Other recent work can be found in the anthology *Black Fire This Time, Vol. 2,* "Why is Monumental Reckoning So Monumental?" and he is currently working on a book with a play "Somebody 'Blew Up' San Francisco State College" about the Black Student Union and Arts Movements that preceded San Francisco State's historic 1968/1969 student-led strike. The project highlights the work done by the students who brought artists LeRoi Jones/Amiri Baraka and Sonia Sanchez to San Francisco State College (now University) in 1966 who helped mentor and help them codify the foundations in which to create the pillars of the first Black Studies Program & Department in the world and the founding of the first College of Ethnic Studies where he is currently an Associate Professor of Africana Studies.

Excerpt from

Somebody "Blew Up" San Francisco State College

Dramaturgical Meditation # 13

That WAS Now, This IS Then

NOTES

The assassination of Malcolm X on February 21, 1965, was a significant moment in the lives of many. Its impact on LeRoi Jones brought forward a revolution in Black creative expression. He abandoned the locations of his collaborations in Lower Manhattan, spewing condemnations towards the lords and ladies of bohemia he was a part of no more. His school, the Black Repertory Arts School was founded in Harlem and opened a month after Malcolm's murder. Two months after its opening it foundered. The Black Student Movement at San Francisco State College (SFSC) knew of LeRoi Jones. Sonia Sanchez was close to Malcolm X. She had left New York in the tumultuous weeks and months following Malcolm's death, met Jimmy Garrett in Mexico, and she ended up at SFSC. She knew LeRoi Jones needed to get out of Newark and New York too. She and Jimmy Garrett, a leader in the growing Black student insurgency movement, also headed the first Black Student Union in the nation. Both inspired, and along with others, invited LeRoi Jones to serve as a guest faculty member/visiting professor in the first Black Studies program. In deference to the invitation, Jones, the poet/playwright and 'artivist,' wrote Madheart, a searing, misogynistic, ritual drama that solidifies the author's emergence as a cultural nationalist. He was an assured man with a calm which camouflaged a subversive vehemence that when paired with anxiousness, emboldened Black revolutionary theatre/communications/media movement through tapping into the hearts and minds of the emergent generation of Black Power seeking youth. The times when he arrived in the Bay Area was when powerful changes were afoot. Madheart, which he also directed, received its premiere on campus transforming the spectators while building community enablement. Madheart was performed up and down the California coast.

This excerpt is from a larger living project where I'm writing about the history of the Black Student Movement, the Black Power, Black Education, and Black Arts Movements before the SF State 1968-69 strike while focusing on the interpersonal relationships of these powerful black pioneers. And not only the men. It is the Black women in any era, but in particular during this time that unequivocally transformed it. It is clear there would be no Black Arts Movement, no Panther Party, nothing, without the unwavering commitment of our Black sisters.

Within the interviews, Dr. Garrett extrapolates about LeRoi Jones' homophobia, his genius, his protectiveness, his mentoring of a young Danny Glover, and more about the work for the play Madheart and how it came to be written and performed. One major point he made in describing Jones' play was that LeRoi Jones was, in the mid-late 1950s into the early 1960s, a theater critic, and one of the most important aspects in the founding principles of the Black Arts Movement is the eschewing of European aesthetics and the development of a new generation of contemporary artists that confronts the contradictions of the Black experience in the racist West. LeRoi Jones was immersed in theater which was impacting his community and his aesthetics through the process of constructing theater which articulated a frothing Black national consciousness. During a February 1965 luncheon/news conference (five days before Malcolm X's assassination), following his play Dutchman's successful premiere, he read his scathing New York Times op-ed THEY commissioned him to write but returned it unpublished. He took questions from the all-white press association with a flair for roasting and cajoling most of them. His response to a question about politics and creating theatre received a most cogent reply. Jones said any time you describe the life of a Black person in America it is a political statement.

The following is a dramaturgical meditation evoking a period in time in the not-too-distant future where there are 'young people' who maintain our history of human revolution and are combatants in the war against the LIE, and embodying the Keeper of the Keys. They are the conduits of our past, present, and future. Zacharia is one of them who receives from the revolutionaries their stories and must eternally hold them within his/their Black bodies. These histories cannot be erased.

SETTING: a "war-torn Big-box Store" (akin to a Target or Walmart)
What we can make out is reminiscent of the bottom of a muddy pond. Murkiness slowly gives way to a shadowy, hazy, imperceptive sediment stirred with particles reflecting shimmer. It is difficult to make out what appear to be bodies, but they are clothes. It is dusk, not dawn. We see a young Black man of about twenty years of age, ZACHARIA, entering from center-right. He runs at first but he starts and quickly turns. He hears gunfire far off in the distance, not too close, but not far either. Or is it gunfire? ZACHARIA continues moving backward afraid of what is off stage. The popping sounds, sporadic, get closer. Shafts of light begin to fill the space as we see ZACHARIA is in a large 'big box' store which has been looted or pillaged following a Black Friday melee or a Black Lives Matter Protest, or an uprising, like in Watts in 1965 or Portland in 2020. Zacharia begins whispering a litany of some kind as the gunfire gets closer and thereby louder, so does Zacharia's voice, which crescendos with the gunfire's proximity.

ZACHARIA

(He sing-speaks softly to gradually shouting)I'm Black, not pink. I am LOST on Bandwidth, 'Cause Bandwidth LOST on me. 'Cause he Black, black LeRoi Jones, the baddest blood in my whole damn world! How'd you like a nice Bavarian punch? That'd be nice. Do we still own the night? Do WE? Because your mind is a horrible thing to waste, Meow, meow, meow, meow, meow, meow, (Barks) Don't let this dog out!! (Barks)I'm gonna make the Matter Lives Black, the, Oh Jimmy, hey Jimmy, OH Jimmy Black-cause you must be black...you, Madness, Madbusy,MADheart,1-877-Bars for Black Kidz, 1-877-Bars for Black Kidz, Call Hazy Justworth 8-7-7-Black-Now, 8-7-7-Black-Now. Two all Black patties special cops let us freeze tickles, guns on an unarmed black bruh's bum, (Screaming) Tripping... meet me tripping, I'm the modern stone age man to be! You bettah walk... Trooper Models work...! cover-up...! Walk it, Girl! Walk your ass away from here... Talk to the white lady 'cause the black lady's too tired! Who was the first man to set foot on the North Pole? Matthew Henson, a BLACK MAN, Please leave please leave, please...

>(Silence. A Beat. A very loud, single gunshot rings out. Zacharia, scrambles while checking to see if he's been hit. He falls to the floor performing a soldiers low crawl while looking for 'cover.')

ZACHARIA

Just give me the night. We used to own it, just give it back.

VOICE OFF-STAGE

Zacharia? Zacharia, you need to come round. Zacharia? When, are you? I don't mean "when", I meant when are you coming 'round?' I mean, literally, you know how you get... WHEN are you?

ZACHARIA

(Trying to hide) That's not the safe question and I'm not sure WHEN I am. Part of my name means sword so I can hear the calls of Logunede which means... (Gunfire rings out) See-I hear Ogun as well. Warriors, stand up, he calling you. (He quickly covers up again)

VOICE OFF-STAGE

Okay "Z" . Well, in a way, I'm you.

>(After a beat Zacharia pokes his head out from underneath his secret place. He writhes and unwraps himself from his 'cocoon' and stands up while straightening out his clothes.)

ZACHARIA

Did that war...(points off stage) just a minute ago, end? Some wars, like the one we in, is long... so I know that the revolution hasn't been televised because Mama & Papa Mayonnaise don't want to see it. Never do. That's why I need you to ask me the question. Then I can tell

you when I am. Shit been happening for eons. Why I gotta tell it?
VOICE OFF-STAGE
You know why. You one of the ones. You got all of it in you.... Zacharia is the one who know. Why do you think you been twenty years old for 400 years? C'mon now. You know what happens when you don't let it out... when you don't speak it.

>   (Zachariah spots a small bench lying on its side, he places it upright while sarcastically repeating, under his breath, what he just heard and pulls the bench center, wipes it off, sits down, slowly inhales deeply, and rests into a Lotus or yoga seated, sage-like posture. He closes his eyes.)

ZACHARIA
Let's do this. (He waits) I'm waiting for you to ask me how old I am right now. That's the question, bruh. Are we on the same page? (He opens his eyes) Well? Ask me how old I am right now.
VOICE OFF-STAGE
How old are you right now, goddammit?!
ZACHARIA

>   (Without missing a beat)

That wasn't so hard, was it? (Slowly inhales deeply and hums the song, Jimmy Mack) The Black Student Revolution. Jimmy, Jimmy, Jimmy Mack... Jimmy Garrett's here. (Pause) I'm 79 years old. (And again closes his eyes. His body, voice, and manner changes) My brother LeRoi Jones was not a fighter per se. His ears heard music as jazz formed words that could shake up the insides of Black skulls. In 1959, he introduced my other 'brother,' Wayne Shorter, as a young saxophonist. You see, LeRoi was a critic, but I'll always think of him as a philanthropist. He could detect the precociousness pouring out of Wayne's tenor sax and had this infallible system of recognizing the overwhelming sincerity of young talent like Wayne. He wasn't a scout for talent, nor was he in any way weaponized to elevate his Black brothers and sisters, for I believe that in his mind, we have always been elevated. He saw the cosmos through his ears.

>   (Beat)
>   (He stands, shakes his body loose, clears his throat, and settles back into his sitting position with eyes closed. He slowly inhales deeply)

Okay, now ask again. Ask me again, how old I am and please don't take so long this time.

> (Silence. He opens his eyes to look for an answer)

VOICE OFF-STAGE

How old are you right now?!

ZACHARIA

(His body and voice change, he's now LeRoi Jones) I'm 27, And two years ago, when I wrote the Wayne Shorter piece, I heard his growth as an artist in the stages of his youth imitating his favorite sounds. In the next stage, his technical prowess developed, as well as his sense of composition. And as I wrote then, his role as an innovator. Or, as another brother is gonna write seven years from now, "Black people are not Western. They are Westernized." In this fantastic arc... (abruptly pauses) It's like the natural course for something extraordinary to evolve and innovate- that's how great bebop is. So, the music I see as this "new music" is coming from this country's great artistic achievement. I say these words because Black-American musicians are of the West and nest their culture within the songs and tongues of jazz and blues, no matter where the hell on the map they are- this has the highest meaning to Black people. And in this regard, European anything is irrelevant.

> (Upon finishing the last sentence, Zacharia freezes. He visually examines his hands, again shakes himself out, assumes the meditative position on the bench, inhales deeply, closes his eyes, reopens them, and closes them again. With one hand he gestures to the audience and clenches his teeth.)

(With teeth clenched) Ask me how old I am right now- again.

VOICE OFF-STAGE

"How old am I right now, again?"

ZACHARIA

> (In one motion, he springs up from the bench in a fight- ready position. Then he acquiesces, backing down onto the bench)

Trying to test my resolve, bringing me some bullshit like that. Ask me right or else I'll fight.

VOICE OFF-STAGE

(In monotone) How old are you right now?

ZACHARIA

Well, that's better. (Closes his eyes and he again is Jimmy Garrett)

Hey, Amiri, it's me, Jimmy. I'm 72 years old and I'm at your memorial and my head is bowed. I'm overrun with emotions and memories. I'm gonna pretend you can hear me, although my lips aren't moving. So, I remember you saying everything European is irrelevant... and I can dig that. As I sit here at this... memorial, a lot happened in your life before our glorious collision. I remember reading that piece you wrote in '61, The Jazz Avant-Garde. The way you wrote about music...(chef's kiss). And I know you were going to see a lot of theatre at the time as well, 'cause you wrote about that too. And your gaze... your gaze was silently feeding some deep furnace that you unleashed not when you spoke at something like a party or a gathering- no, it was when you got up on the stage or wrote on the page where you unfurled this elegiac wrath that kidnapped my imagination, as I'm certain you did with so many others. Here's the thing, now this is popping into my head... I need to break this down since I'm here, sitting in this pew, staring at my Florsheim's... I know you saw Genet's The Blacks because we all had something to say about it. And we did talk about the Theatre of Cruelty, the Theatre of the Oppressed, and your favorite, Ritual Theatre... I bet you never knew this, but I totally understood that—

VOICE OFF-STAGE

(Interrupting) --what did you totally understand?!

ZACHARIA

(Continuing unperturbed) You wrote this one little play, Madheart- it wasn't so little- you were writing at the same time I was experiencing the uprisings in Watts... and your fire-breathing prose mirrored that tumultuous terror, that thorn in the lion's paw that caused all of us to scream primally "muthafuckas, get your boot off my neck!" (He laughs) Well, we got you to the San Francisco State College campus and we were already raising Cain. Unbeknownst to us, you had written this play and in one fierce moment, I remember you shoving that script into my jaw, with that narrow-ass index finger pointed to the role of Black Man, and then shoving that same finger into my chest. Every brother on campus, from towering Danny Glover to the brawny Muscle Shoals Alabama Agamemnon's who wanted that part and had time to do it—but no, you chose all five foot nine of me.But since I did take that role, here I am, able to communicate with you and prognosticate how I know what is to come and to be renewed by what has passed—because that was now, and this is then. Amiri, this isn't a judgment call or anything, but I can see no way around all of that theatre not prickling at that furnace inside of you and there's nothing from other people's creativity that we haven't borrowed. Our human revolution is pre-ordained because of what we can transform into our voices. You were everywhere. You saw, heard, and touched this world of bohemia. You were with Ginsberg and O'Hara. You even saw Genet's work as it premiered. You were feet first in that 'pot of viddles' and there was no way you were gonna come out with your porous creative life not being impacted by all that you saw, heard, and felt. You were irradiated, my brother.

        (Beat. Zacharia freezes eyes wide open. He stands up abruptly
        and carefully listens for any sound. He squints.)

(In his voice) Did somebody just laugh? They best not have because this temporal shit ain't easy. I'm an artist and I'm sensitive about my shit.

        (He returns to the bench, shakes himself off, and then resumes
        the meditative position with his eyes closed. He slowly inhales
        deeply.)

VOICE OFF-STAGE

Well, how old are—

ZACHARIA

        (ZACHACARIA gestures sharply to silence the voice)

Shush! (He's back to his meditative position) I'm still 72. So Amiri, you and me, we're these sponges, right? And I mean, we've remained friends for so long that even this trivial reflection strikes me right now as curious. I was remembering all of these discussions with you about the word "faggot" and your incessant need to use it every other sentence… not just by you. But I'm reflecting and I remembered our brother-in-arms Ed Bullins when he told us Black folks not to go see The Blacks. And he said Genet was a "French pervert" with "faggoty ideas about Black Art, Revolution, and people," and you agreed with him. Because of the times, all of us Black men as artists who were fighting for revolution, and it was brothers like Eldridge who drew the line in the sand and publicly chastised all of us for not being "fit for duty." And so all of a sudden, the homophobia became part and parcel, and coming from you and Brother Bullins and Stanley Crouch, I always found it disingenuous because I knew all of you too well. Since I'm sitting here at your memorial, staring at my Florsheims, I guess I don't have to reiterate my persistence about you using that word as generously as you often did—but I digress.

(ZACHARIA stands and begins acting out what he's saying.)

So, Amiri, remember this? "Good evening Ladies & Germs, our main desire is to entertain you. So, we have murdered this white lady. She's right over there." Do you... remember? And of course, you remember this: like in The Blacks, the white characters are played by people with Black skin wearing white masks, remember? Am I ringing a bell? No? Check this out: "Lights up, the DEMON LADY- "(whispering as an aside) the white lady- "recumbent in the center of the space with a lance, stuck in her abdomen and another in her enchanted area."

(ZACHARIA continues 'performing' as Jimmy Garrett)

"You are forever to be unalive, and will have died because I yearned for it, you will remain the essence of death, or the frigidity of its efficacy and the rocks of its guarantee." (Acting out his words) And I then lurch forward, plunging my stave into her heart, and then thrusting it down into the floor below. "Wondrous. Wondrous," I cry out.

(ZACHARIA moves about, happily)

So there you have it, Amiri, two distinct plays that open with the death of a white woman. One is written by a "French pervert," and the other by the instigator of the Black Revolutionary Theatre. You found your ritual theatre within the ritual theatre of a Frenchman. That's all. I'm saddened you're gone, this memorial is boring. Knowing folks still say our names... means they remember you as...

(Jimmy Garrett, vanishes, as ZACHARIA appears)

...I do. Unrelentingly.

VOICE OFF-STAGE

(Frustrated) Are you through yet? How old are you now?

ZACHARIA

(He crosses to the bench and sits down)

That's a good question.

(End Scene)

Jimmy Garrett

Jimmy Garrett is a former SNCC worker and student at San Francisco State College. He was a pioneer of the Black Campus Movement. Garrett arrived at San Francisco State in the spring of 1966 with the intention of relocating the Black Student Movement he had participated in the last six years (as a member of SNCC and CORE) from the community to the campus. In the next two years, more than 90 percent of the sit-in demonstrations by Black students occurred on college campuses in 1967 and 1968.

Garrett also conjured up the idea for the discipline of Black Studies—an idea that soon circulated throughout the nation. After leaving San Francisco State in 1968, Garrett co-founded and served as the director of the Center for Black Education in Washington D.C. and he was one of the principal organizers of the 6th Pan-African Congress in Tanzania in 1974. Over the last several decades Garrett has stayed active in the struggle for human rights, earning a law degree and doctorate in political philosophy and sociology of education along the way. His play, *And We Own the Night*, first was performed as a part of the 1967 Black Communications Project at the Fillmore Auditorium in San Francisco, where writer LeRoi Jones directed the production.

And We Own the Night: A Play of Blackness

We are unfair
And unfair
We are black magicians
Black arts we make
In black labs of the heart

The fair are fair
And deathly white

The day will not save them
And we own the night.
—LeRoi Jones

Characters

JOHNNY
LIL'T
MOTHER
BILLY JOE
DOCTOR
TWO BLACK YOUTHS
TWO BODIES

The scene is an alleyway, dark, dirty, dingy. A large trashcan sits stage right next to a red brick building. The entire rear of stage right is a line of buildings shaded and faded, red or brown brick or graying white wooden frames. A dim yellow light sits above the building closest to the front of the stage. To the left of the stage is a tall white picket fence, also graying. To the right of stage front, around the trashcan, is a broom, leaning against the building. At the very rear of stage left lies a dead BODY: a black youth. In the center rear of the stage is another BODY, a white man dressed in a policeman's uniform.

The lighting should give an effect of dimness, not darkness though it is night, of muted light, of soft shadows, of a kind of grey dinginess. The time is that of the present and that of death and dying.

From off stage there is the sound of gunfire, in short bursts, then in a long sustained burst, followed by high shrilling sirens. Then more gunfire.

VOICE, *offstage.* Johnny's been shot! Help me!

SECOND VOICE. Is he hurt bad?

FIRST VOICE. Yeah, get a doctor, Billy Joe.

SECOND VOICE. Okay. I'll try to find his mother too.

FIRST VOICE. To hell with his mother. Get a doctor, dammit. We'll be in the alley behind Central Street.

Two young black men enter from stage left as if from behind the fence. Johnny, tall and thin with fine black features, is being crutched by LIL'T who is small-statured and has a high brown face. They move toward the building at stage right.

LIL'T. Come on, Johnny, sit here. *He props Johnny up against the building in front of the trashcan. JOHNNY is clutching his left side where his shirt is covered with blood. He is holding a pistol in his right hand.*

JOHNNY, *breathing heavily.* Lil'T . . . Lil'T . . . Bad . . . Mother . . . fuckin' cops . . . *Clutches* LIL'T . . . caught us from behind . . .

LIL'T. They won't fuck with nobody else. I blew 'em away.

JOHNNY. Good . . . Good . . . *Grimaces, then clutches LIL'T.* Lil'T, find mama.

LIL'T. Cool it, Johnny. Don't talk, brother. *He touches the wound.* You're bleedin' like hell. The doctor'll be here in a little while.

JOHNNY. No . . . find Mama . . . Tell her . . . Stay away. Tell her stay home. Ain't no . . . women here . . . Tell her . . . Lil'T.

LIL'T. Don't worry Johnny. We'll keep your mother away. She knows we got a war to fight in this alley. She knows we're kickin' the white man's ass.

JOHNNY. Naw man . . . She ain't . . . She ain't . . . no good . . . that way . . . keep her away . . . til we win . . . then she'll understand. Not now . . . not yet . . . *He nods his head from side to side.*

LIL'T. She can't stop us Johnny. Nobody can. The white man can't. Your Mama can't. Nobody. We're destroying the white man. There's wars like this in every big city . . . Harlem, Detroit, Chicago . . . all over California. Everywhere. We've held off these white motherfuckers for three days.

JOHNNY. Yeah . . . If we can keep pushin' . . . we'll win . . . we'll win. Keep Mama away . . . Keep her away . . . til we win. I'm scared. I can't fight her and the white man too. *He clutches his side and grimaces.*

LIL'T. Cool it brother . . . You the leader Johnny. You ain't scared of nothing, everybody knows that. You're smart. You know how to fuck to whitey. You fight too hard to be scared of a woman.

JOHNNY. You don't know. Lil'T. You don't know . . .

LIL'T. What you mean, I don't know. I've known you for three days . . . three days of fire. I know how you fight . . .

JOHNNY. No. You don't know. On the street, in the alley, I'm a fighter. But in my mama's house I ain't nothin.

LIL'T. What you mean?

JOHNNY. She's too strong. She about killed my Daddy. Made a nigger out of him. She loves the white man . . . She'll take me home.

LIL'T. Home. This is home. This alley and those bodies. That's home. I'm your brother and you're my brother and we live and fight in alleys. This is home. And we'll win against the white man.

JOHNNY. We're brothers.'T but mama believes the white man's God. *He lapses into silence nodding his head from side to side.*

LIL'T. Cool it Johnny. Don't be so uptight. Where's the fucking doctor?

VOICE, offstage. Go for soul! LIL'T turns his head toward stage left and rises. A short, stocky, black faced young man enters. A rifle bangs loosely at his shoulder.

LIL'T. Where's that doctor, Billy Joe?

BILLY JOE. I got him. I found him hiding at his home. Come on in the alley, Doc. A little dirt won't hurt you.

DOCTOR *enters, crouching low moving slowly, passes* BILLY JOE *toward* LIL'T, *who is standing. He looks around as if expecting to be shot. He is a light-complexioned Negro in his late forties, dressed in an expensive-looking gray suit.* LIL'T *goes over and jerks him forward.* BILLY JOE *leaves.*

LIL'T. Come on, Doc. We ain't got no time to be jiving. Johnny's bleeding bad.

DOCTOR, *standing above Johnny.* I don't . . . I don't know what I can do.

LIL'T, *raises his gun.* Man, you'd better do something quick. DOCTOR *leans over* JOHNNY *and kneels.*

DOCTOR. That boy rushed me so quick I didn't get a chance to get my tools. I just stuffed what I could in my pockets. *The* DOCTOR *presses the area where* JOHNNY *is bleeding.* That's a bad wound.

JOHNNY. Aw. *He slides away from the* DOCTOR. Be cool, man.

DOCTOR. Be still, boy, or you'll bleed to death. *Two* BLACK BOYS *rush on stage from the right, one carrying a pistol, the other a rifle.*

FIRST BOY. Lil'T. *He stops to catch his breath.* The cops've broken through the barricade on Vernon.

LIL'T. Which barricade? What happened?

SECOND BOY. The one on Vernon . . . The cops come in buses, five of 'em.

FIRST BOY. Yeah, looked like fifty cops a bus. The cats saw all them cops, an' ran.

LIL'T. Where'd the cats go? Up to the park?

FIRST BOY. Yeah, they set up another barricade.

SECOND BOY. We got to think of something or them cops'll break that 'un too. We came to get Johnny. He'll know what to do.

LIL'T. He can't move. He got shot lil' while ago. *The* TWO BOYS *turn to go over to* JOHNNY, *but are held up by* LIL'T. Naw, man, don't bother him

. . . He's been hurt bad. Wait til the Doc's finished.

FIRST BOY. Man, we can't wait. *They rush over to* JOHNNY. *The* FIRST BOY *kneels in front of the* DOCTOR, *the other stands behind him.* JOHNNY *rolls his head around.* Johnny, Johnny. Wake up brother Hey, what's wrong?

DOCTOR. I gave him something to kill the pain.

SECOND BOY, *kneeling, grabs* JOHNNY *by the arm.* Aw, fuck. Wake up Johnny.

LIL'T. Whyn't you cats leave him alone. *Moving over to the group.*

JOHNNY. Oh. Oh. Waking. What Wha . . . Lil'T. Lil'T.

LIL'T, *kneeling.* It's all right, Johnny. These cats . . .

FIRST BOY. Look, Johnny. We know you hurt but we need your help, man. Them cops're rushing the barricades in buses. Hundreds of cops.

SECOND BOY. Man. We got to stop them buses or they'll wipe us out. Cats ran from Vernon. They're all the way down the park now. Got another barricade goin'. But it won't hold long!

DOCTOR, *as* JOHNNY *sits up listening.* Wait a second. I'll be through with this bandage in a minute.

JOHNNY *to* DOCTOR. Yeah, yeah. Look here. Throw broken glass in the streets. Then pour gasoline up and down the street for a block or so. If the glass don't stop 'em, plant cars in places so they can hide with fire bombs. An' when the buses get in the middle of that gasoline, chunk them bombs under 'em.

FIRST BOY. Roasted cops!

SECOND BOY. Wow! Oh, man . . . outta sight. Outta sight! Come on. Let's go. We'll get 'em. Go for soul Thanks Johnny. You're a heavy cat. *They exit.* Go for soul!

DOCTOR. Boy, if you don't be still, you'll bleed to death.

LIL'T. He's right, Man. Ain't no use in you cuttin' out on a humbug. You blowin' too much soul. BILLY JOE *enters.*

BILLY JOE, *to* LIL'T. I saw Johnny's mother down at the barricade.

LIL'T *takes* BILLY JOE *to the side of the stage left.* She's not coming here is she?

BILLY JOE. Yeah, man. I told her to come. I thought Johnny might die. I thought his mother should . . .

JOHNNY. Lil'T . . . Get this dude off me.

DOCTOR, *turning to face* LIL'T. I'm just patching him. He's restless.

LIL'T. It's okay, Johnny. Take it easy Doc. *Back to* BILLY JOE. Look man . . . We got to keep his old lady away . . . She's a bitch. Johnny don't want her around. Go keep her away.

BILL JOE. But. She's his mother . . .

LIL'T. I don't give a shit. Keep her out of here. Go on. *Pushes* BILLY JOE.

BILLY JOE. Oka man. *He rushes out.*

LIL'T *turns toward* JOHNNY *and the* DOCTOR.

VOICE, *offstage.* Look out son. You nearly knocked me down. Where's my son at? Where's Johnny at?

BILLY JOE, *backing on to stage.* You can't come in. Lil'T says you got to stay out . . .

JOHNNY'S MOTHER *enters, backing* BILLY JOE *into the alley. She is an imposing black woman, wearing a simple dress of floral design and flat shoes. She never smiles.*

MOTHER. Boy, don't you mess with me. Where is my son at? *As she speaks,* LIL'T *turns. He is blocking* JOHNNY *from his mother's view.*

BILLY JOE. I don't know where the dude is. *Realizes he is in the alley and stops.*

LIL'T, *walking toward them.* I told you to keep her out.

BILLY JOE. I . . .

MOTHER. Johnny! *She rushes over to* JOHNNY *and kneels, pushing the* DOCTOR *out of the way.* BILLY JOE *shrugs his shoulders and leaves.*

JOHNNY. Mama. Mama. Go back home.

DOCTOR. Don't shake him woman! He's been shot. He's bleeding inside.

MOTHER. My son. He's my son. *She speaks loudly but does not sob.* You the doctor? Will he be all right?

LIL'T, *clutching the woman by the shoulders and trying to lift her*. He's all right. Come on now. Billy Joe'll take you home.

MOTHER, *jerking loose*. Naw. Let me go. Who are you? Why'd my son get hurt like this? You're the cause of it.

LIL'T. He got shot by a white cop.

JOHNNY. Go way Mama. T get her out of here.

MOTHER. Don't you talk to me like that. You bad boys. Sinning. And this is what you get. *Points at* JOHNNY'S *wound*.

LIL'T. Ain't nobody sinning but the white man. Now he's payin' for it.

MOTHER. Johnny layin' there bleedin' and the white man's payin'. Help me doctor. Help me take him to the hospital.

JOHNNY. Mama leave me alone.

LIL'T. Johnny ain't goin' to no white man's hospital. Them motherfuckers would just let him die.

MOTHER. Don't you curse white people like that. Doctor help me.

DOCTOR looks up at LIL'T who has lifted the gun. No we shouldn't move him. I've slowed the flow but he's still bleeding internally. He'll die if he moves around too much.

MOTHER. But he can't stay here in this alley. Oh lord help me, what can I do?

DOCTOR. I've got to get that bullet out quick. I'll go back to the office and get my case.

LIL'T. Okay Doc. Billy Joe can take you and make sure you get back. Billy Joe? *DOCTOR rises*. BILLY JOE enters. Take the doctor back to get his stuff.

BILLY JOE. Okay, come on, Doc. *They leave*.

MOTHER. Is it bad son? Is it bad? Oh Lord. What can I do? I need strength.

JOHNNY. Mama, don't pray. It don't do no good.

MOTHER. I told you to stay home. Out here fightin' the Police. Burnin' down white folks' businesses. I'm ashamed of you. God knows why you're doin' this.

JOHNNY. I'm bein' a man. A black man. And I don't need a white man's God to help me.

MOTHER. What you say? What you say 'bout God?

JOHNNY. Forget it.

MOTHER. Where'd you learn all that stuff. *She rises and turns to* LIL'T. Did you teach him this sacrilege?

JOHNNY. Nobody taught me.

LIL'T. He's leader. He knows how to fuck with whitey.

MOTHER, *to* LIL'T. Boy, can't you talk without cursin'? Don't know child like you need to talk that way. To JOHNNY. Your daddy's a man, and he don't curse.

JOHNNY. Where is he, Mama?

MOTHER. He's at home where you should be 'stead of out here in this alley.

JOHNNY. Is he hidin', Mama?

MOTHER. Naw he ain't hidin'. He's just stayin' close to his home.

LIL'T. While his woman's out on the street. Bullshit. A man don't need to hide. Can't. He'd be out here fightin' like us.

MOTHER. You're wrong boy. God knows you're wrong. You out here breakin' laws. Killin'. Look at what you've done. *She points at the bodies lying on the stage.*

LIL'T. People die when they face the white man. Better to die like a man, bringing the white man to his knees than hidin' at home under a woman's skirt.

MOTHER. My husband ain't no sinner. He don't break laws. He works hard . . . He don't bother nobody. He . . .

JOHNNY. He's still a nigger.

LIL'T. He believes what the white man says.

MOTHER. You don't know him. You don't know what he believes.

LIL'T. Be a good nigger, work hard, pray, kiss ass, and you'll make it.

MOTHER. How do you know? How do you know?

JOHNNY. I know, Mama.

MOTHER. I'm gonna take you home. Away from this sin.

JOHNNY. Don't bother me, Mama.

MOTHER. I brought you into this world. I clothed and fed you. And now you don't want me to touch you? I'm taking you home. *She tries to lift* JOHNNY. LIL'T *rushes over and grabs her by the shoulder, pulling her away.*

MOTHER. Let me go. *Breaks away from his grip.* Don't put your hands on me again.

LIL'T. Well you leave Johnny alone. Can't you understand? He's a man. He's a leader. He's my brother. We're gonna stay here in this alley and fight the white man together. Right Johnny?

JOHNNY. Yeah, brother.

MOTHER. You ain't no leader, boy. You ain't even got no mind. *Turns to* LIL'T. He's got the mind. A dirty mind. Why don't you leave him alone? He's just a boy. He didn't know about hatin' and killin' til he started running with you.

LIL'T. Killin' ain't no dirty thing to do to a white man.

MOTHER, *rising.* Murder ain't never been clean.

LIL'T. Except when the white man did it, right?

MOTHER. Who are you, the devil? I ain't speakin' of the white man as you call it. He ain't done me no harm.

LIL'T. He beat you and raped you. He made a whore out of you and a punk out of your man.

MOTHER. Naw. The white man ain't done nothing to me. But I don't know you. Where are your folks?

LIL'T. My mother and father are dead. They died the first day fightin' the cops. My brother's in jail. My sister's somewhere fightin' or dyin'! My home is this alley and Johnny is my brother. This where I live or die.

MOTHER. You don't have nothin' left. You don't feel nothin'. You ain't found God. You don't have love.

LIL'T. That God you pray to is a lie. A punk. The last dick the white man't got to put in you.

MOTHER. You see, Johnny. He's got no heart. He's got no love.

LIL'T. Love! Love! Everybody knows that love ain't enough for the white man. He don't understand love. You got to kill him. Love! Ass suckin' love. Askin' him for forgiveness when he'd done wrong. Lettin' him shoot you in the back while you're on your knees prayin' to his God.

MOTHER. Jesus said . . .

LIL'T. Another punk . . .

MOTHER. Jesus said love those who are spiteful of . . .

LIL'T. Strokin' his rod, cleanin' his shit . . .

MOTHER. Forgive those who do harm . . .

LIL'T. Blowin' up black children in churches . . . Beatin' pregnant women . . .

MOTHER. We must pray to God for salvat . . .

LIL'T. Kill that motherfucker! Cut out his heart and stuff it down his throat. Bury him in his own shit.

MOTHER, *quietly, slowly.* I will not strike out at white men. They have been good to me. Fed my son. Gave me shelter when there was no work for my husband. Gave me a job so I could care for my family. White men have done me no harm. Only niggers like you trying to take my son away and lead him to sin.

LIL'T. The white man gave you a job and took away your husband's balls. You have the money and your husband's a tramp in his own home. Ain't that right Johnny?

MOTHER, *to* JOHNNY. *She speaks quietly at first, then building to the end.* Johnny. Son. In God's name, you know how I love you and your Daddy. How I've worked and slaved for you all. And you know how white man's folks have always helped us. They're smart. They know what's right and what ain't. We got to trust in them. They're good. They run the whole world don't they? How come you're out here killin' white men. I don't understand. Livin' in this filth. Crawlin' around alleys bleedin' to death. You call yourselves men. Don't no men act like that. The white man don't crawl around, cussin' and stealin'! You ought to be actin' like the white man 'stead of tryin' to kill him.

JOHNNY, *tries to rise.* Mama . . .

LIL'T. Sit still Johnny. You'll start bleedin'.

JOHNNY. I'm already bleedin'. *Tries to rise. He gets to his knees and stops, breathing heavily. LIL'T starts toward him, then stops.*

MOTHER. Don't try to get up son.

JOHNNY. Just stay away . . . I'll make it . . . I should try to be a white man, huh? White as snow. White as death. Don't you wish I was white Mama. Clean and white like toilet paper.

MOTHER. Johnny . . .

JOHNNY starts to rise from his knees. He is holding the pistol with one hand and clutching his side with the other. And Daddy. Don't you wish he was white too? Daddy's smarter than I thought he was. He had to decide between bein' a white man and bein' nothin' and he decided to be nothin'!

MOTHER. Sit down Johnny, you're bleedin'!

JOHNNY. So I'm bleedin'. It's blood comin' from a black body shot by a white cop. Or don't that matter?

MOTHER. You were doing wrong.

JOHNNY. The white man decides what's wrong. The white man's right no matter what he's done. Right Mama. I'm wrong from the time I was born. You love the white man. And I kill the white man.

MOTHER. You made yourself into a criminal.

JOHNNY. My name is criminal. I steal and kill. I am black and that is my greatest crime. And I am proud of that crime.

MOTHER. I didn't raise you to be no criminal.

JOHNNY. You raised me to be white, but it didn't work. The white man is my enemy. I wait in alleys to stab him in the back or cut his throat.

MOTHER. But that is heathen.

JOHNNY. I have been a heathen for three days. He has for three hundred years. But I am not guilty. I feel passion when I kill. Love. He don't give a shit for nobody. He kills efficiently. I kill passionately. He is your God and I have sworn to kill God. Can't you understand, Mama? We're gonna build a whole new thing after this. After we destroy the white men. Black people don't want to kill. We want to live. But we have to kill first. We have to kill in order to win.

MOTHER. But you can't win. They've got guns and bombs. *Loud explosion. They all stop—startled.* God, what is it?

JOHNNY. It's the police buses, they got to the police buses.

LIL'T. Blow them motherfuckers away! I'll go see. *He leaves stage right. As soon as he is out of sight a second explosion roars. He rushes back on stage jumping wildly.* Boom! Man, Johnny, you should have seen that scene.

JOHNNY. Are they gettin' to 'em?

LIL'T. Goin' for soul. Gimme five brother. *He extends his open palm to* JOHNNY *who takes his bloody left had away from his side and slaps* LIL'T's *palm.*

JOHNNY. See. See mama. We're winnin'! *Dabbing his side.*

MOTHER, *quietly.* I don't see nothing boy 'cept you lost your mind. There's nothin' I can do with you. *A third explosion.*

LIL'T *rushes up to* JOHNNY *and spins him around seemingly not remembering that JOHNNY has been shot.* Forget her, Johnny. She's too old. JOHNNY *spins around with* LIL'T, *stumbling but trying to acquiesce to the dance.* This is judgment day, and we're the judges. Motherfuck the police. Motherfuck the white man. JOHNNY *is stumbling, holding the gun and clutching his side.*

JOHNNY. And motherfuck daddy and mama and all them house niggers. Death to the house niggers! *A fourth explosion.* JOHNNY *tries to dance and falls to his knees.* It's all over for the white man, huh T?

LIL'T. You damn right. *He picks up his rifle.* I'm going out to the barricade. I ain't gonna stay and wait for that Doctor no more. We got a war to fight.

JOHNNY. Okay, brother, be cool.

LIL'T. *Walks up to* JOHNNY *who is breathing very heavily while his body falters.* I hope you don't die brother . . . But you know how death is. It's over with. Ain't no more after that. Gimme five. *He extends his hand.* JOHNNY *slaps it with his last expression of strength.* LIL'T wipes the blood onto his shirt and leaves, not looking back.

JOHNNY. Mama . . .

MOTHER. You ain't my son. I don't know you. You rejoice when you kill white people and don't even feel sympathy for each other when you are dying. That boy did more toward killin' you than any white man but you love him.

JOHNNY *falls forward bracing himself by his elbow.*

JOHNNY. Mama . . .

MOTHER. Don't Mama me. I don't care about that no more. You steal and kill and curse God. You call yourselves criminals and feel no remorse. You hide in alleys cuttin' throats. You blow up buses and burn down property. That boy left here knowin' you'd die and he was smilin'. I don't understand. He'll probably be dead himself in a few minutes. I just can't see it. I know you're wrong. The white people would never do those things. You must be wrong. I don't understand. They'll make it right. They'll explain it to me. They'll show me the way. I trust in them. Ain't no nigger never been right. *She turns slowly and walks toward the stage left.* And never will be right.

JOHNNY *points the gun at her back.* We're . . . new men, Mama . . . Not niggers. Black men. He fires at her back. *She stops still, then begins to turn.* JOHNNY *fires again and she stumbles forward and slumps to the stage.* JOHNNY *looks at her for a moment, then falls away. There is a loud explosion followed by gunfire.*

LUCINDA ROY

Lucinda Roy is an Alumni Distinguished Professor in Creative Writing at Virginia Tech where she teaches in the MFA program. Her awards include the Eighth Mountain Poetry Prize for *The Humming Birds* and the Baxter Hathaway Poetry Prize for her slave narrative "Needlework. Her work has appeared in numerous publications and anthologies.

Madonna in the Bush

A woman carries water on her head.
The way she moves is function's nod to form.
Watching her I know what I once knew:
walking is as close to god as prayer.
The bush around us pulses, swirls, and falls
as energy and matter paint the dark.

Unnatural is the soul who fears the dark
when shadows are a habit of the head.
That which propels us to rising has to fall.
What is there to see with if not form?
Uncertainty's a principle of prayer
and *Beauty* is a word I thought I knew....

Strange how we lose the things we knew
and reinvent the subject in the dark.
Observation is an alternate path to prayer
but who can escape the clamor in the head
when all sight is seen, all beauty bound to form?
Beauty is the way a bare foot falls

on a dust-blush path in the bush where fall
is as distant as mirrors, and a woman knows
the weight of the child on her back—his form
conforming to hers, his dark their dark.
The word for *mother* beats inside her head.
Motherhood is devotion—this the prayer.

Need and wish and hope give birth to prayer.
We brace ourselves against the pull of fall.
The woman carrying water on her head
perceives a world the likes of me can't know.
Balance is to movement what shadow is to dark—
the only words worth knowing are the ones we form.

The busy world I live in seems devoid of form
and migration is the route I take from prayer.
I forget to wonder what's inside the dark—
a body falling can't perceive the fall.
Yet I believe there's something mothers know
holier than the noise inside my head:

a woman's form can alchemize the fall
and prayer is sight's homage to what is known—
beauty dark enough to balance light upon its head.

Credits

James Baldwin, "Amen" and excerpt from *Blues for Mister Charlie*, reprinted from *Black Fire This Time* (2021). Aquarius Press, www.WillowLit.net.

Jimmy Garrett, *And We Own the Night* reprinted from *Black Fire This Time Volume 2* (2024). Aquarius Press, www.WillowLit.net.

Nikki Giovanni, "No Complaints" and "Rosa Parks" reprinted from *Black Fire This Time* (2021). Aquarius Press, www.WillowLit.net.

devorah majpr, "downpressors", "city values" and "writing love" reprinted from *califia's daughter* (2020). Aquarius Press, www.WillowLit.net.

Lenard Moore, "Summer Blues for George Floyd", "8 Haiku" and "Haiku Sequence" reprinted from *Black Fire This Time* (2021). Aquarius Press, www.WillowLit.net.

Denise Nicholas, excerpt from *Freshwater Road* reprinted from *Black Fire This Time* (2021). Aquarius Press, www.WillowLit.net.

Ishmael Reed, "The Luckiest People in the World" reprinted from *Black Fire This Time* (2021). Aquarius Press, www.WillowLit.net

Lucinda Roy, "Madonna in the Bush" reprinted from Fabric (2017), Aquarius Press, www.WillowLit.net.

www.ingramcontent.com/pod-product-compliance
Lightning Source LLC
Chambersburg PA
CBHW051235210726
48290CB00003B/972